MISTAKEN FOR LOUD COMETS

Mistaken for Loud Comets

lily someson
Introduction by Tony Trigilio

Winner of the Spring 2021 Host Publications Chapbook Prize

Copyright © 2021 Host Publications

All rights reserved. No part of this book may be reproduced in any form or by any electronic or mechanical means, including information storage and retrieval systems, without permission in writing from the publisher, except by reviewers, who may quote brief passages in a review.

ISBN: 978-0-924047-93-0
ISBN short: 0-924047-93-3

Book Design: Claire Bowman
Cover Design: Annar Veröld

Published by Host Publications, P.O. Box 302920, Austin, TX 78703

www.HostPublications.com

CONTENTS

Introduction x

how to write to your inmate 1

concerning the ufo sighting near edinburgh correctional facility 2

poem made of my father's letters to my mother, 2004–2014 3

there is a scientific study that suggests suffering is genetic 4

hazard reduction 6

"lisa, i saw so many geese coming out of a dark grey cloud" 8

there is a scientific study that suggests suffering is genetic					10

self-portrait as my mother at her heaviest weight					12

creation myth					14

nar-anon					17

there is a scientific study that suggests suffering is genetic					18

when my college roommate asked *is your mother black or white*—					20

my great-grandmother considers her immigration to chicago, 1909					22

In 1910, in one of the first formally recorded instances of police brutality in Chicago, a police officer shot a Black child playing with his friends mistaking him for a robber. The police later explained, "the boy was probably large for his age."					24 [my father calls me his daughter and i search] 25

[i want to say i found my father's letters]   27

there is a scientific study that suggests suffering is genetic   28

release poem (bird-watching)   29

poem in which my little brother asks about Tamir Rice   30

portrait of house with visitor   31

References   34

Acknowledgments   36

INTRODUCTION

Lily Someson's poems break down walls and free us to imagine a world without confinement. They're driven by an urge to re-envision coercive language and social structures in the name of empathy, encouraging us to look out for ourselves and for each other—to nurture the communities we are born into and the communities we have chosen. Freedom is more than just an abstract concept in *mistaken for loud comets*. Instead, in poems thick with detail, Someson dramatizes freedom as something tactile, a physical and psychological practice that can be cultivated even within social systems that do everything in their power to keep us contained.

Someson offers a necessary reminder that nothing, not even captivity, can diminish our kinship bonds. Her poems emphasize that writing itself, as a practice of attentiveness and intimacy, can resist the degrading gestures of all the disciplinary regimes in our lives—the prison system, to be sure, but also the carceral networks of systemic racism and cis-heteronormative gender and sexuality. Someson creates a liberating voice from the tension between the will to punish and the will to live free. The state prison system instructs its letter writers, "do not / write anything in the letters that you wouldn't want a third party to read," and seemingly in the same breath it commands: "do not ask your inmate to hold you / without permission from the prison." Against this dehumanizing logic, Someson composes poems of love and dignity for her incarcerated father, along with moving explorations of the kinship bonds of her extended family—poems that invite us to consider the meaning and value of our own individual communities. How do you write "your inmate"? How do you even begin to respond to a system that deliberately reconfigures "your father" as "your inmate"? Someson suggests that you write to make your memories palpable—to remember, always, the person whom the state wishes to submerge with the word "inmate." She writes, "do / not send flowers because your inmate has forgotten what they look like," adding, crucially: "do not forget   your father / do not forget   your inmate."

The poems in *mistaken for loud comets* craft a language for freedom while subjected to the extraordinary pressures of the United States' out-of-control prison system, a carceral network designed to punish inmates rather than to rehabilitate—and to extend multigenerational punishments to inmates' families. A culture's ethos can be judged, of course, by how it treats its most vulnerable, especially those whose freedoms the state has authorized itself to take away. The deprivations and separations of the prison-industrial complex, its deliberate cruelties, unfold with frank, tactile honesty in these poems. But this book does more than catalogue the cruelties of absence and isolation. Instead, Someson creates a counter-discourse based on caretaking, community, and empathy. In his "A Defense of Poetry," Percy Shelley writes that poetry strengthens the faculty of empathy "in the same manner as exercise strengthens a limb." Someson's poems empathize with those who have been othered by a dominant culture's disciplinary mechanisms. Her work reinforces the idea that we are greater than our worst mistakes—we are, first, members of a human community, and our transgressions, whether large or small, do not define who we are. As Audre Lorde writes in "Poetry Is Not a Luxury," such a socially informed poetic practice is vital to imagining a future world of equity and compassion: "it is through poetry that we give name to those ideas which are—until the poem—nameless and formless, about to be birthed, but already felt." Someson's poems enact what is "about to be birthed, but already felt," guiding us to measure our lives not by profit margins or consumption, but instead by how we sustain and nurture ourselves and our communities. In this way, *mistaken for loud comets* functions as a superbly crafted, vivid, and emotionally powerful instruction manual for opening the heart and mind.

As these poems explore family histories framed by race, gender, sexuality, and immigration, a vision of a more communal world emerges. When you write to "your inmate," you dissolve the plexiglass separation between yourself and your loved one. You choose the human being over the human system, even as the carceral network imposes tremendous obstacles on the fundamental human contact required, simply, to be. Someson's poems imagine the liberating possibility of second chances. They envision rapturous new beginnings, a "sky ballet" of "orange birds of paradise dotting the horizon," a world where penitentiary plexiglass does not prevent human touch. These are poems of vision and possibility—the most necessary poetry of all.

Tony Trigilio
December 2020

The function of freedom is to free someone else.
— Toni Morrison

For Dad—my whole life, may we meet in these pages

HOW TO WRITE TO YOUR INMATE

do not use staples or paper clips within your letter to your inmate   do not use marker, crayon, glitter, glue, stickers or lipstick on the letter or envelope addressed to your inmate   do not give your inmate drawings or markings that can be misconstrued as secret code i.e. art, pictures, children's drawings such breaches in security will result in destruction of the letter   do not ask your inmate to hold you without permission from the prison   do not speak of the way freshness is always heavier in the mornings as your inmate has not seen the dew in so long   do not forget your inmate   do not write anything in the letters that you wouldn't want a third party to read   do not learn anything in childhood that your inmate was meant to teach you since it will not be the same without them   do not send flowers because your inmate has forgotten what they look like   do not talk of the outside world in your letter   do not talk of your new life   do not think that someone will love you   that anyone will love you   without becoming trapped in some thing or another, their arms outstretched and waiting   do not forget   your father   do not forget   your inmate

CONCERNING THE UFO SIGHTING NEAR
EDINBURGH CORRECTIONAL FACILITY

suddenly at dusk everyone's fathers
float out of their jail cells all locs grown long again
their concrete ceilings opened up beaming
towards the heavens it's some sort of
rapture floating wildly above our heads unidentified
objects orange birds of paradise dotting the horizon father as in
sky ballet father as in never in the wrong place
at the wrong time boots lofty like there is so much to celebrate
all of the police have never seen a gun
they don't say a damn thing fathers doing somersaults
shackles nowhere men mistaken for loud comets
midwest america pointing upwards   *look, a second chance,*

a doppler of white light, some blinking oblivion to witness
and tell our children about

POEM MADE OF MY FATHER'S LETTERS
TO MY MOTHER, 2004–2014

remember when we were   not old, still brandished with   our own touches?   we went to lake michigan off of miller beach and it was back when the sand   was still so visible and unrelenting, licking the inside of its own stomach   remember? and you wore   those white capris   you know the ones;   your hair was so   long i thought i could never find my way   out of it, the coils wrapping themselves   around themselves and it was so   early i thought that maybe   if i never took my eyes off of you the whole day it would never   get darker, the morning fading into its own   pseudolight and long dance and you would   never have to leave. i think it was 1994,   and i swear lisa   i swear i've never seen anything more beautiful   than you on that day when we met and   i just knew we would have so many more days like that, so yellow and   quiet and holy and i know   i'll get out of here sweetheart and someday we can go back and relive   our mistakes   like i never did a bad thing   like i was never   anything but lover and lover and father and and   someday we'll touch not through the plexiglass, its shape bowing under   our heated palms   and every day   every day   we'll turn 30

THERE IS A SCIENTIFIC STUDY THAT
SUGGESTS SUFFERING IS GENETIC

i did not see the gun   but i did see the small mountain of skin that it left   his chest
a tilled earth   a mound of steel thrust beneath the surface

no i did not see the gun but i saw   the aftermath of it, the way my father
thumbed the wound around his heart   when speaking, as if feeling it

always for the first time
please   don't make the mistakes

that i did   his fragile means of protection   a hailing
of metal   banging   banging   in my small hands

a shell   an example   and i want to know who tried
to unmake him   to wedge something foreign

4

where a muscle should be   who missed his funeral by one fraction
of an inch

my father   found that death
was always pressed against the window   watching. now it won't stop

sulking toward him   slow   salt lick of purgatory.   the shallow hum of his voice—
please   are you listening?

the sound of a buck   shot in the field for being   large
and alive.   the grass, a heavy sound   like mockery, though i am

less majestic   i was born into   that same familiar warmth   a wetness
in the torso   crows circling the house   my father, never learning

from their calls   the black night always.

HAZARD REDUCTION

we are picking corn husks from her car wheels, my mother
double gemini, her four angled faces hovering, car propelled
off of 700 north, mid-august crop
eating the paint from the thing it took her
ten years to pay off.
staring at wreckage, i'm tired
of how passive i am, sitting on
the garage recliner, waiting
for her to call—

she's hiding cigarettes in her breast pocket
as i ask her if she ever wanted to get married. she steals candy
from the walgreens, places pots on the floor
to catch leak, though they always overflow, won't tell me
about her DUI until three years after the fact. we look
towards each other as if both wishing

to be mothered, our eyes never meeting
for more than a few seconds, wheel always
off-kilter, a large wreck
to come back and tend to.

"⌣ MANY GEESE COMING OUT ⌣ARK GREY CLOUD"

after the poem my father wrote for my mother

i must ask
if you care that i saw them, too. birds

black feathered, flung astral and heavenward, carving the air
hard with their bodies.

my mother pretends she has not seen them, maybe,
but i've always waited for their ascension, followed

them down route 20 until everything was
winged and disastrous. these geese

disrupt everything, these geese fly
through the poem, the exosphere, demand

to be touched by the hand of god
or whatever's closest to it, paternal

and otherwise. you call and ask for my mother
but i can't admit that i, too, have come out of something

grey and cumulus, a thing
who cannot love you correctly. your voice, paternal

and otherwise, asks me to write more letters, but i am
suddenly her, just rounded at the edges, softer

and more willing to listen.
my lisa, where have you been? i am hurried at the mention

of her name. here we watch as grief reroutes the sky, makes everything
push back out.

when the birds finally drop through the air
they all wear your face

THERE IS A SCIENTIFIC STUDY THAT SUGGESTS SUFFERING IS GENETIC

he was almost genius-level, my mother laughs to herself, *but always*
humble about it. she tsks through the phone receiver.
Matt was your dad's brother, but he felt too saintly to be
related to anyone. she recalls a heavenly body, before the thick
of summer swallowed him useless. *he loved you.*

i do remember him, gentle hands beveled by work, skin
the color of garden soil. *we never knew*
how sad he was.   a silence over the line. i don't want her to say it,
don't want to give the poem

a blood supply. i'm tired of mentioning fluid, how its
maroon covers everything. i never meant to imply
that we all survived, my uncle becoming a reminder that facts
cannot be rewritten. i too have clutched
the barrel of something, have wished that all things
would become quiet. i cannot blame his exit, the blue

of his favorite suit at the service, the way i used to plan
who would get the rest of my things. my mother sighs
through the phone. *your dad's brothers all had such unhappy endings*. i ask
if she has ever known why.

SELF-PORTRAIT AS MY MOTHER AT HER HEAVIEST WEIGHT

in the photo there is the girl   wide nose pushing her face forward, angular,   arms clutched tightly against an old boyfriend, cheeks flushed my mother   is 22, hair rolled perfectly up towards god her lips red and cinched back, a face like blinds being pulled upwards,   laughing with my eyes, the mirror of our bodies   ripe hip, plum-like and glittery,   holding friction in all the same places   and i wish so badly to stop here   to look at joy   to see how its hands are clasping a lover's waist, how its earrings are huge, fabulous and unreasonable,   a sequined jacket catching violet light   brilliant under a disco ball, our legs filled out with party favors, apple picking, how that girl looks straight into my eyes like she knows me already,   knows that i will carry burden in my wrists like she does, will attempt to lose joy and gain it back again   like my mother who is not yet a mother, not yet knowing the weight of her future, banging hard against dinner plates   which is to say that the night my mother stepped on a scale, vowing to lose 100 pounds one summer,   attempting to lose our same-bodies, her meals medicated and sparse,   strangers asked if i was adopted despite our hands, identical in size   leaning up against opposite sides of a mirror whispering *i hate you,*   *i hate you*   her bones without marrow   small birds, a tower of stacked joints and i see her now,   how she stares back at me,   my shrunken twin,   my own shape widening   gently, as if to soften a blow

CREATION MYTH

when i came out to my mother i cried
in the garage low and silent in her arms i was twelve

and barely knew what *pansexual* was save my frantic
internet searches, let alone how to explain that to this ghost

woman as she stared through me, her eyes empty in confusion
finally musing, *when you put it that way, I guess*

that's what I am too and *everyone's a little gay* and my mother,
that last-minute thunderstorm suddenly came out to me

in a flurry of surprise and the next morning in church i watched
her crane her head back in the pew

with swan-neck, staring at the preacher as her eyes fluttered in
and out of sleep. in my smallness i mimicked

her face, the way her features fastened onto this man of the lord,
this crystallized southern baptist who sang about glory,

God's wrath—who spat about sin and banged his fists on
wooden pulpit and above him the portrait of christ

that was suspended high in the air shook as he talked about our
eternal damnations

and my mother leaned into me with simply *don't worry about him* but that unreachable portrait

of jesus, painted white and innocent, continued to bore his gaze
through me in the third pew as she glanced down

nervously at her lap and that day, while i wouldn't dare admit it,
if you were there God,

i could never look you dead in your face

NAR-ANON

i dream of you healthy this woman
who does not answer her phone on mother's day.
woman who has my hips, swollen knee, who went
to miller beach to watch the meteor shower.
woman who has never married, who never wanted
to be controlled, who cries at forrest gump while
ignoring her children.   i love you, stupidly,
like a light that has burnt out—
go to the bathroom with your purse, pace around
the house, hide the shoebox under the bed.
hollow-boned and sunken, you float in and out
of your body. how i fantasize about making you
a reality, an intervention of angels—
how i turn on porch lights and watch you
like a hawk near the medicine cabinet.

THERE IS A SCIENTIFIC STUDY THAT
SUGGESTS SUFFERING IS GENETIC

my doctor is asking
about chin hair, sexual

tendencies, the details of how my head splits often
in ache. most days

my ovaries throw themselves
against the hallways of my body. *Too much testosterone*

my doctor concludes—he examines my palms, uterus
decorated in cysts, hips slanted

under a microscope. *Are you more
tired than usual?* a female frame

with the mirror broken inside of it. i consider
when i have binded my chest

to itself in protest, hormones so comfortable
orbiting masculine. i know

nothing of my own heat, testosterone
flooding the office, the waiting room, rushing

around my anatomy—body always hurling
against itself, begging god

to let it be everything, to let it be everything
all at once

WHEN MY COLLEGE ROOMMATE ASKED *IS YOUR MOTHER BLACK OR WHITE—*
she pressed until i gave in, sliding my skin under a microscope. *I knew it—all pretty mixed people*

        have white moms. cornered, she dissected me into an experiment, brought me
        the sterile knife and tray, assumed that the palatable parts of a body were gifts

from a white womb.   *Black women*, she said, were *too calloused to create pretty children*,
perpetual suffering on our faces. in our dorm i was the only Black

        body, which is to say
        voiceless and awake. *your eyes seem caucasion, maybe. but your nose—*

she mulled over my face like staring through drawn windows, a voyeur plotting
how best to exploit. i desperately wanted to become simple and translucent, a pointed nose

        with high cheekbones, like my mother

        white orchids plucked from her spine. how easy it would be

to wake in a body with that mask of whiteness, how my roommate assumed
she was giving me a compliment, as i looked in the mirror

        to my new half-reflection.

MY GREAT-GRANDMOTHER CONSIDERS HER IMMIGRATION TO CHICAGO, 1909

it was a bad year. a spotty winter with days
tied up in their own racket. all of my boys cry out
in the squeezed hours of the evening, a clanging in the living room,
colliding themselves in wood burned   half-light. is it too late
to say we've made a mistake, taken our brood
too far from a land that once nurtured us,
from my mother   who is too far to write. around the table
we speak of the old country, swaddled in hips
and children, our language
deadweight in my mouth, consonants
lulled and stuttered on my documents. what is this america
that has cracked my good plates, beat
the dust from my frock, stowed me
in ship manifests? i have dreamt
of chicago like my hand was on
a trigger, like my boys playing in the steel yard,

melting january in my salt-teeth.
how *americănesc*. what is romantic
about my shined broach, my fear
of water after the journey, my collection
of sons: two worlds
haphazard on their breath

IN 1910, IN ONE OF THE FIRST FORMALLY RECORDED INSTANCES OF POLICE BRUTALITY IN CHICAGO, A POLICE OFFICER SHOT A BLACK CHILD PLAYING WITH HIS FRIENDS MISTAKING HIM FOR A ROBBER. THE POLICE LATER EXPLAINED, "THE BOY WAS PROBABLY LARGE FOR HIS AGE."

o city of broad shoulders, o special boy of long limbs, city that my grandmother built, i have grown taller than other boys in my grade, full face made of down feathers, wooden soldiers, i thrash my arms in the air with fluorescence, filled with sweets that mother gives me before bed, my brothers shining under porchlight, playing with masks, pretending to be things they are not, i am always outgrowing my church vest, swollen and joyous, my brothers dancing around me, steel mill fathers looking up, and suddenly i am forty feet tall, the rain like creation, skyline as likeness, towering the ferris wheel, doves perched on my ears i am cradling everything above me, hands always reaching, copper and glimmering, i hear sirens below

[MY FATHER CALLS ME HIS DAUGHTER AND I SEARCH]

my father calls me his daughter and i search
for what i wish he meant, *my kin my family my*

daughter is too closed a word, each letter
abstract in its placement, his mouth

claiming me female like it was all too fated
to argue. i shrink at the sound of it, the consonants

heavy in the mouth. in our first
phone call in fourteen years he mentions

how he loves my voice, how i sound
just like my sister my mother my

speech is not worthy of theirs, masculine in its
clutch and inflection, a pink room

i am locked out of. i have died
so many times, a light erupting

into prisms of self—
if i tell him the girl he left is no longer alive

it will become
true, will become another

bloodletting, a body to collect and
come home to

[I WANT TO SAY I FOUND MY FATHER'S LETTERS]

i want to say i found my father's letters underneath my own mouth
in the midwest house, all curled up and chewed from years of reading
and going over. i want to say they meant something more
than words. this is not the story everyone wanted, the truth
churning itself all over the kitchen table, all over the
frantic sky. my father appears and we are in a room where we can exist
at the same time without so much thinking about it. i'm having the dream
where he has nothing to say except for that the sunlight looks so
bright from the window above us, like he hasn't felt its heat
in years. i want to tell you the story without feeling like
i need to prove that he says anything.
he tells me about my own name
like he owns it in his mouth, like he made it with his hands
out of the glass separating us, the barelythere of it all.
i do think he says *tell your mother i love her*
and i can never remember what i say after that

THERE IS A SCIENTIFIC STUDY THAT
SUGGESTS SUFFERING IS GENETIC

on the phone from prison my father asks
if i am happy. every conversation
yields the same ache. how can i say
that i'm not, that i take everything
for granted while he stays frozen
in plexiglass through this life
and the next. i outlive him
over and over again in my poems, write
the eulogy, mourn loud and send his body
to the lake. while he is alive i cannot
speak to him normally, a tooth shocking
in absence. i will always tell him
that i'm the best i've ever been.

RELEASE POEM (BIRD-WATCHING)

black birds tap against the kitchen window, tails sputtering
toward the earth. i haven't seen these before—dark-eyed juncos
from my research—little round snowbirds, snug bodies packed on top
of the power lines. i am intimidated by their sameness, their conformity
in flight. my father knocks against the glass. none of this should be happening.
i turn my face from them, decide i like the word *junco*, say it softly while making
breakfast, weaving a butter knife and thinking of bird bellies flashing
like frantic stars. my therapist suggests that i should write about my father
like i am piecing together lost artifacts. grief is turning away from the kitchen window
and seeing a stranger wearing my face, the birds perched on his wide shoulders
as he sits on my bed. i turn my face from them, but i tell you my father is out of prison
because it's true, not because it makes him more real. the juncos are perched on the sill now,
staring through glass. i marvel at their proximity.

POEM IN WHICH MY LITTLE BROTHER ASKS
ABOUT TAMIR RICE

i do not want to write the poem. i do not want to make the comparison, though it's right there—do not want to talk about Black death, though it's right here. instead, the poem takes my brother to an ice cream shop, to marquette beach, down the boardwalk to inspect the large expanse of sky against lake michigan. the poem takes my brother home and helps him with homework, buys him new school supplies, considers algebraic formulas, points out wrong answers. later the poem gives my brother a pat on the back, a little spending money, and an unlimited supply of apple-cider doughnuts. and maybe the poem buys him a brand new wardrobe of anime shirts, cozy pants, and a lava lamp. later the poem will beg my brother to get rid of his hoodies, beg him to leave the nerf guns at home, remind him to not play outside after dark. the poem will say *i cannot lose you,* and the poem may lose him.

PORTRAIT OF HOUSE WITH VISITOR

I invite my father to sit down
in the poem. I ask him if god exists
in captivity. I invite him into my space
which is to say we are near one another
for the first time. I would like to build a room
without a steel mouth. I invite him in, holes
in his pants, punctured stars. A room with a stained
glass window, we talk about normal things

like normal people. A breakfast nook, then. Little salt and pepper shakers,
a kitschy tablecloth. I ask, *Are the windows too small?* He whispers,
to be Black is to know death. He was in solitary for six months. My face,
uncanny valley as he struggles to look at me. Our noses are the same, carved flat
on round faces. I build. Make the house bigger, less claustrophobic. I paste him into photo albums.
A living room, then. A vintage chaise lounge, orchids on the coffee table, decadence. In the house he
talks slowly, measuring his life. They cut his locs

in prison. In the poem they're still there, but we have to pretend. He is twenty years younger, we paint murals in the living room, we cook his mother's recipe for cornbread, we fight over the remote.

We bicker about the news like real people do. I build him new locs, a new head for them to rest on, a body that was born free. I sew his pants, corduroys worn from walking, gardening, going to the store for milk. I'm playing god. We're still in the house, remember? We have to pretend. I paint the poem white with blue shutters. I choose the furniture for him to sit on, a new bed, white sheets with purple violets, no metal in sight. I build a poem around him, a world without confinement. Yellow light through a screen door, the outside mocking us with its magnitude.

REFERENCES

"concerning the ufo sighting near edinburgh correctional facility" is a reference to the Sufjan Stevens song, "Concerning the UFO Sighting Near Highland, Illinois." This poem also references Edinburgh Correctional Facility, which is the prison where my father was held for the last part of his sentence.

Both "poem made of my father's letters to my mother, 2004–2014" and "nar-anon" reference Miller Beach, a neighborhood of Gary, Indiana.

"there is a scientific study that suggests suffering is genetic" is a sequence of poems inspired by an emerging scientific theory that explores the possibility that a human's DNA can be altered by emotional trauma, causing transgenerational trauma in their children.

The second sequence poem of "there is a scientific study that suggests suffering is genetic" is inspired by the poet Aaron Smith.

"nar-anon" is a reference to Nar-Anon Family Groups, a 12-step program for friends and family members who are affected by someone else's narcotic/opioid addiction.

"my great-grandmother considers her immigration to chicago, 1909" includes the word *americănesc*, the Romanian word for American.

"In 1910…" was created with gathered research from "A History of Police Violence in Chicago" by Livia Gershon. The poem is inspired by the line "City of the Big Shoulders" from "Chicago" by Carl Sandburg.

"poem in which my little brother asks about Tamir Rice" has a reference to Marquette Park Beach, which is a beach on Lake Michigan in Gary, Indiana. The poem also references Tamir Rice, a 12-year-old victim of police brutality from Cleveland, Ohio. May he rest in power.

ACKNOWLEDGMENTS

I am eternally grateful for my family, whose fierce kindness and understanding have been my guiding force through this process: Gran, Pop, Matthew, Mom, Uncle Eddy, Katie, Rhen, Teppy, Dan, Coco, Uncle John + family, and Uncle Curly. I could never thank you all enough for the graciousness you've given me throughout my life.

For my closest friends: Drew, Thair, Liz, Abrina, Eli, Emme, and Skylar. Thank you for being my support system and chosen family.

For the Chicago and Nashville poetry communities, and all of the wonderful poets within who have supported me throughout the creation of this manuscript: Jess Mascarenas, mo santiago, Doe Parker, Scott Strom, Ayla Maisey, Gillian Marwood, Rye McFarlane, Cassie Calcaterra, Kay Thompson, Vic Peralta, Zoe Joslin, Talia Wright, Rivka Yeker, Lemmy Lempert, Rosie Accola, Sage Aliaga, Kiyoko Reidy, Caroline Stevens, John Mulcare, Hayes Cooper, Jessica Lee, Maria Isabelle Carlos, and anyone else who has shared their bright light and knowledge with me throughout this time.

For my dedicated mentors: Jenny Boully, David Trinidad, Jenn Morea, C.M. Burroughs, Lisa Fishman, Kate Daniels, Rick Hilles, and Robin Mosley-Vaughn. Thank you for the countless office hours and your close attention to my work. An extra special thanks to Tony Trigilio for writing the foreword of this book, and for showing me over and over again what compassionate leadership looks like.

For the Host team, who worked tirelessly and selflessly so that this book could be out in the world (and became my close friends along the way): Annar Veröld, Claire Bowman, and Joe Bratcher.

And of course, for my loving partner, Sav: thank you for your late nights, unwavering warmth, fierce dedication, keen eye, and abundance of patience. You are my constant.

Further acknowledgments for the generous editors who published some of the poems in this book:

Academy of American Poets: "portrait of house with visitor"

I Scream Social Anthology, Vol. 2: "self-portrait as my mother at her heaviest weight," "hazard reduction," and "my great-grandmother considers her immigration to chicago, 1909"

Columbia Poetry Review: "there is a scientific study that suggests suffering is genetic" (2)

Hooligan Magazine: ' "lisa, i saw so many geese coming out of a dark grey cloud" '

Court Green: "how to write to your inmate," "i want to say i found my father's letters," and "poem made of my father's letters to my mother, 2004–2014"

This book is dedicated to my beautiful aunt, Susie Thomason, and to my father, Larry Darnell Jones, neither of whom could be here with us for its release, but who are here in constant and glorious spirit. This is for Chicago, for Lake Michigan, for Black lives, for incarcerated mothers and fathers, for the brave activists who defend them, and for you.

Thank you.

THE HOST PUBLICATIONS
CHAPBOOOK PRIZE

Our chapbook prize embodies our values as a small, community-oriented press by elevating the voices of women writers. The prize awards publication, $1000, 25 copies of the published chapbook, a book launch at Malvern Books, and national distribution with energetic publicity and promotion.

lily someson (she/they) is a poet and essayist from Chicago. She has obtained a B.A. in Poetry from Columbia College Chicago and is a winner of the 2020 Eileen Lannan poetry prize with the Academy of American Poets. She has read at the Poetry Foundation's Open Door Reading Series and has also been published/is forthcoming in *Court Green, Queeriosity* (Young Chicago Authors), and *Columbia Poetry Review,* among others. She is currently a first-year Poetry MFA student at Vanderbilt University and an assistant poetry editor of the *Nashville Review*.